James Bond Themes
for Easy Piano

Cover photograph courtesy of Rex Features

ISBN 978-1-78305-427-5

HAL•LEONARD®
CORPORATION

7777 W. BLUEMOUND RD. P.O. BOX 13819 MILWAUKEE, WI 53213

Visit Hal Leonard Online at
www.halleonard.com

The James Bond Theme

Music by Monty Norman

swing

Em⁷

4

Goldfinger

Words by Leslie Bricusse & Anthony Newley
Music by John Barry

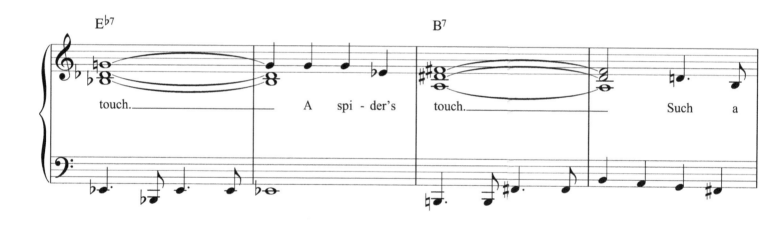

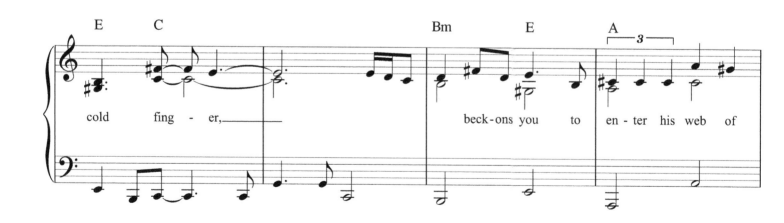

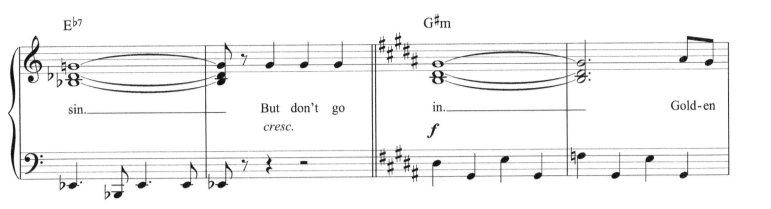

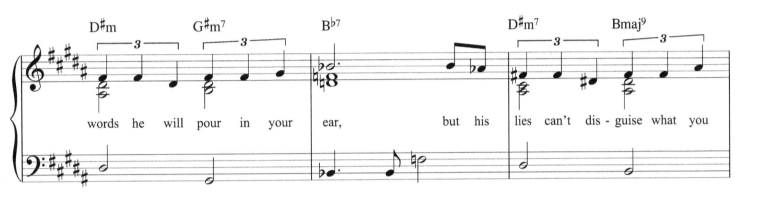

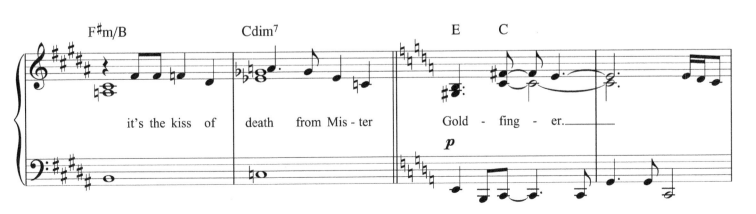

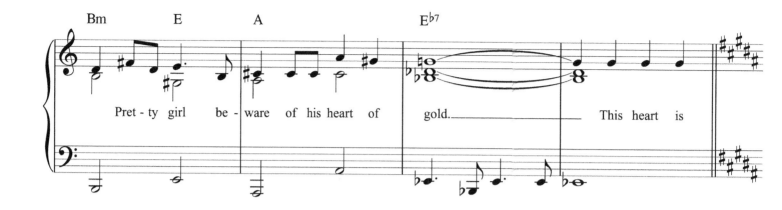

Bm · E · A · E♭7

Pret-ty girl be - ware of his heart of gold._____ This heart is

G♯m

cold._____ He loves on - ly gold._____ On - ly

gold._____ He loves gold._____ He loves on - ly gold._____

G♯m⅚

___ On - ly gold._____ He loves gold._____

You Only Live Twice

Words by Leslie Bricusse
Music by John Barry

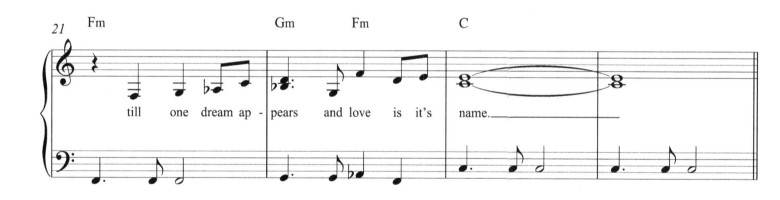

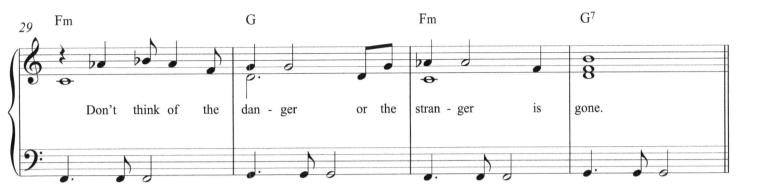

Don't think of the dan - ger or the stran - ger is gone.

This dream is for you so pay the price.

mp

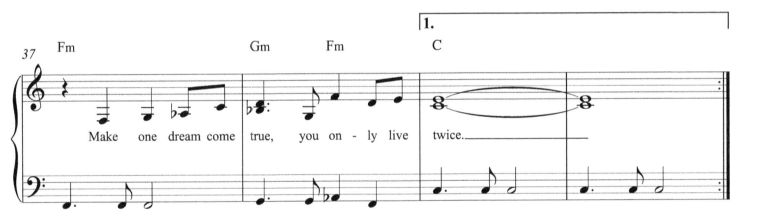

1.

Make one dream come true, you on - ly live twice._____

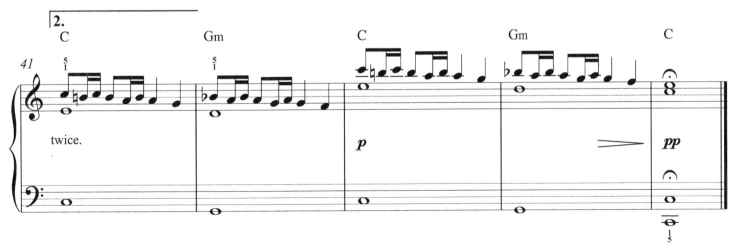

2.

twice.

p

pp

11

We Have All The Time In The World

Words by Hal David
Music by John Barry

13

Diamonds Are Forever

Words by Don Black
Music by John Barry

Live And Let Die

Words & Music by Paul & Linda McCartney

Live and let die,___ live and let

die,___ live and let die.___

ff

mf What does it mat - ter to ya,

when you got a job to do___ you got - ta do it well,___ you got - ta

19

give the oth - er fel - low hell!

Nobody Does It Better

Words by Carole Bayer Sager
Music by Marvin Hamlisch

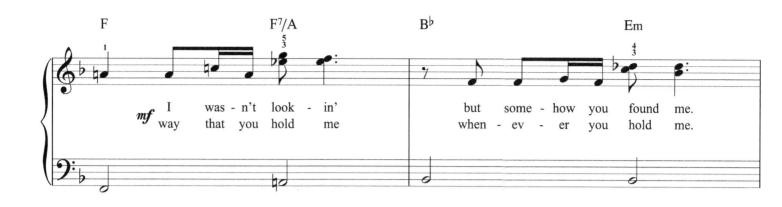

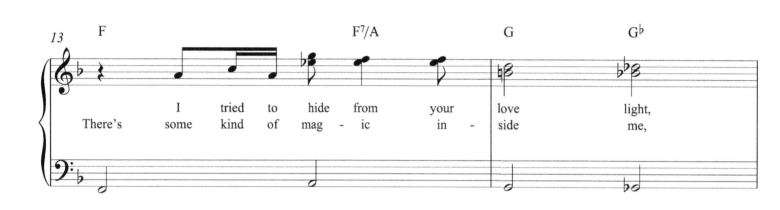

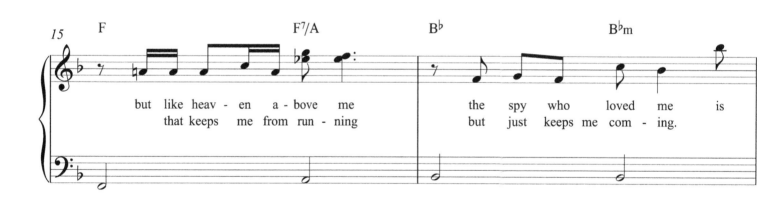

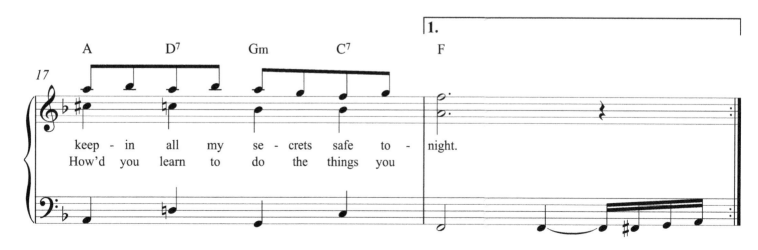

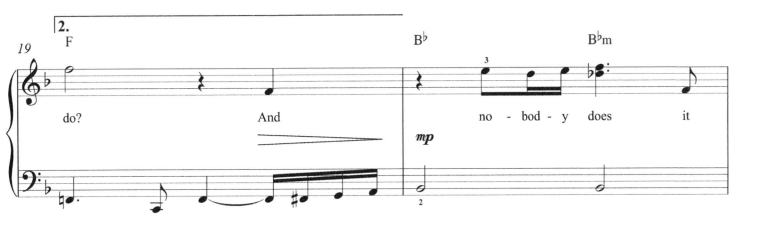

do? And no - bod - y does it

bet - ter_____ makes me feel sad for the rest.

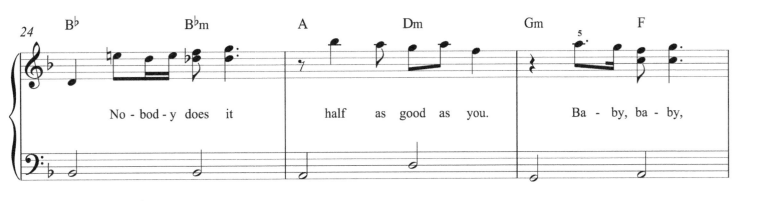

No - bod - y does it half as good as you. Ba - by, ba - by,

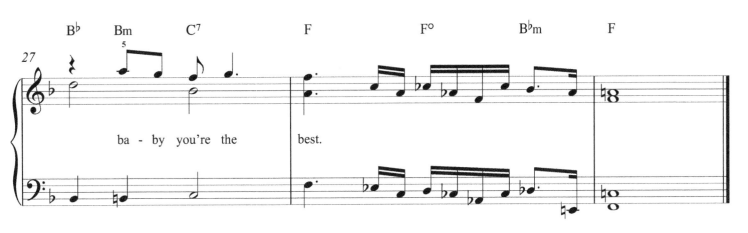

ba - by you're the best.

Moonraker

Words by Hal David
Music by John Barry

1. Where are you? Why do you hide?
2. Where are you? When will we meet?

Where is that moon - light trail that leads to your side? Just like the
Take my un - fin - ished life and make it com - plete. Just like the

Moon - rak - er goes in search of his dream of gold,
Moon - rak - er knows his dream will come true some day.

I search for love, for some - one to have and hold.} I've
I know that you are on - ly a kiss a - way.}

seen   your   smile   in   a   thou - sand   dreams.   Felt   your

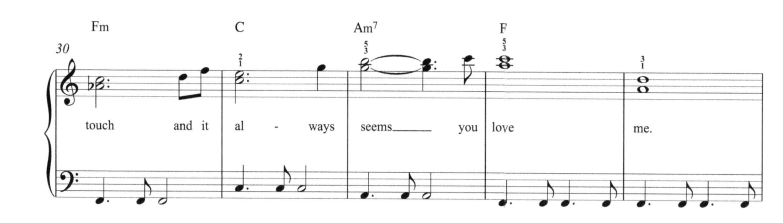

touch   and   it   al - ways   seems_____   you   love   me.

1.

You   love   me._____

2.

me._____

For Your Eyes Only

Words by Michael Leeson
Music by Bill Conti

love, I know you need-ed me, the fan-ta-sy you freed in me.
pas-sions that col-lide in me, the wild a-ban-doned side of me.

1.

On-ly for you.___ On-ly for you. *dim.*

2. For

2.

On-ly for you.___ For your eyes on-ly.___ *dim.*

p

All Time High

Words by Tim Rice
Music by John Barry

Licence To Kill

Words & Music by John Barry, Leslie Bricusse, Anthony Newley,
Narada Michael Walden, Walter Afanasieff & Jeffrey Cohen

1. Hey, ba - by, thought you were the one who tried to run a - way.
2. Hey, ba - by, think you need a friend to stand up by your side.

Say that some-bod-y tries___ to make a move on you,

in the blink of an eye___ I will be there too.

And they'd bet-ter know why I'm gon-na make 'em pay

till their dy-ing day,___ till their dy-ing day,___

till their dy-ing day.___ Got a

Tomorrow Never Dies

Words & Music by Sheryl Crow & Mitchell Froom

41

The World Is Not Enough

Words by Don Black
Music by David Arnold

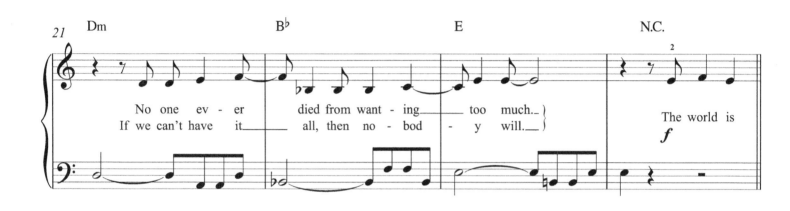

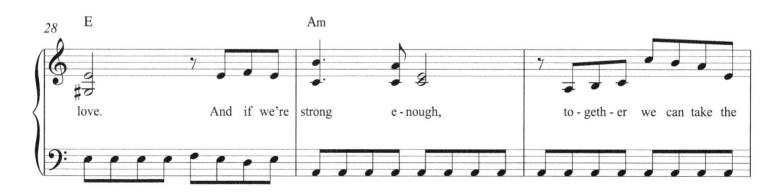

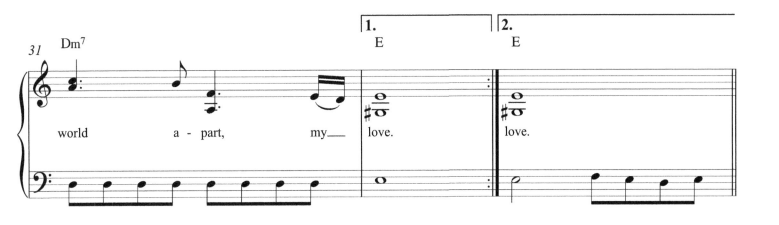

world a - part, my___ love. love.

I feel sick;___ I feel scared;___

I feel read - y,___ and yet un - pre - pared. The world is

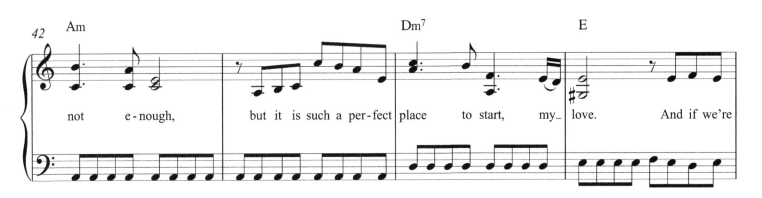

not e - nough, but it is such a per - fect place to start, my_ love. And if we're

strong e-nough, to-geth-er we can take the world a-part, my

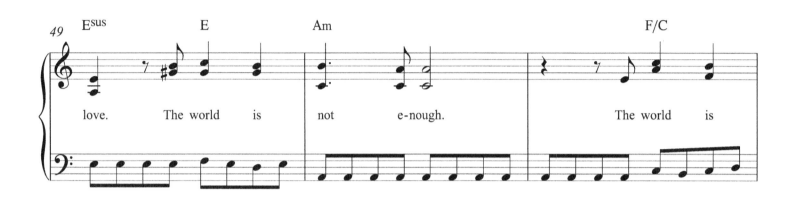

love. The world is not e-nough. The world is

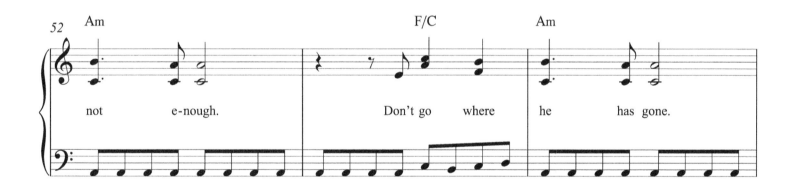

not e-nough. Don't go where he has gone.

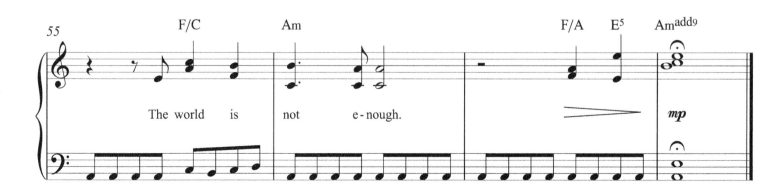

The world is not e-nough.

You Know My Name

Words & Music by David Arnold & Chris Cornell

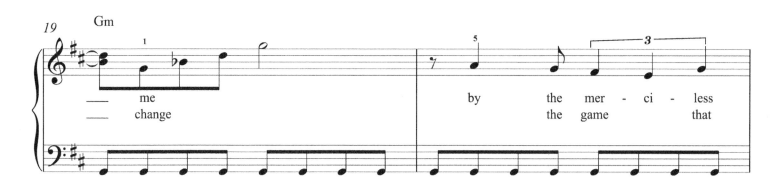

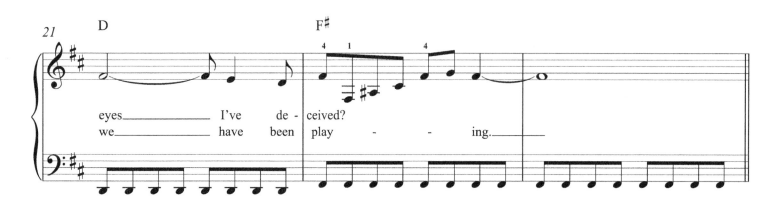

Skyfall

Words & Music by Paul Epworth & Adele Adkins

123456789